At the Heart

At the Heart

New Selected Poems

Charles Taylor

Copyright © 2011 by Charles Taylor. All rights reserved.

ISBN: 978-0-9835968-3-7
Library of Congress Control Number: 2011935971

"Citizens" appeared in *Voices* 2010, 74
Cover photo by Charles Taylor
Cover design by Tommy Alan Raines

Manufactured in the United States

Ink Brush Press
Temple and Dallas, Texas

This book is dedicated to those who believe in the mysteries of the heart and in the mystical divine at the heart of the heart.

Recent Books from Ink Brush Press

Jerry Bradley, *The Importance of Elsewhere*
Ashley and Nathan Brown, eds. *Agave*
Laurie Champion, ed., *Texas Told'em*
Terry Dalrymple, *Fishing for Trouble*
Terry Dalrymple, ed., *Texas Soundtrack*
Millard Dunn, *Places We Could Never Find Alone*
Chris Ellery, *The Big Mosque of Mercy*
Andrew Geyer, *Dixie Fish*
Andrew Geyer, *Siren Songs from the Heart of Austin*
H. Palmer Hall, *Into the Thicket*
Charles Inge, *Brazos View*
Dave Kuhne, *The Road to Roma*
Myra McLarey, *The Last Will and Testament of Rosetta Sugars Tramble*
Jim McGarrah, *The End of an Era*
Karla Morton and Alan Birkelbach, *No End of Vision*
Robert Rynearson, *Time to Listen*
Jim Sanderson, *Dolph's Team*
Jim Sanderson, *Faded Love*
Steven Schroeder, *a dim sum of the day before*
Steven Schroeder, *a guest giving way like ice melting*
Jan Seale, *Dearness Happens*
Jan Seale, *Nape*
Jan Seale, *The Wonder Is*
William Seale, *Texas Riverman*
Melvin Sterne, *Zara*
W.K. Stratton, *Dreaming Sam Peckinpah*
Charles Taylor, *Saving Sebastian*
Caroline Watanabe, *My Many Sisters*
Jesse Waters, *Human Resources*

Learn more about these and other books at www.inkbrushpress.com

Tis a gift to be simple,
tis the gift to be free,
tis the gift to come down where you ought to be
And when we find ourselves in the place just right,
It will be in the valley of love and delight

Shaker Elder Joseph Brackett, Jr. (1848)

"I want to be free of poetry's ornaments."
    —Anne Waldman, "A Phone call from Frank O'Hara"

CONTENTS

Introductory Note   xiii

I. Place To Begin

Place to Begin: Bryan/College Station	1
They Grow, They Go	3
Dogmen	4
Plain Song	7
Photograph of My Brother	9
Sketch of a Friend	11
At the Heart of the Heart	13
Mother Ann	14
Virge's Vigil	16
Parenting	17
Boy in War Beirut	18
Terror Infirma	19
Futurology	22
Homesick	24
For Akemi	25
The Suicides	27
No Ambition	29
Be Here Never	30
Miracles	31
Marx, Brother?	32
Words are 4	33
Excuses	35
So It Goes	37
Lies of History	39
This Child	41
American	42
Ancestor	43
I feel a better	44
Home	45
Dear Reader	47
On the Assassinations	48
Oneida	50
One Answer	52
In Time	53
The Stranger, The Mystery	54
So Much	55
Keep It Easy	57

Moment	58
Conundrum	59
Albert Schweitzer	61
A Day	62
To See Anew	63
Tsukmimi	64
Key	65
Memo To Sensei	66

II. The River Runs

On Learning	69
Death Dream	70
August Morning	72
1949, Oregon	74
Punishment	76
Song for the Buddha, Bubba	79
The Blind Man	81
Love	83
Sister God	84
Taking on the Big One	85
King Debs	87
The Coming	89
You Get It	90
Odd Attitude	91
Brazos Valley	92
Word play, Make Way	93
Fundamental	94
Auto Elegy	95
Transvestite	97
Man Alone on His Porch	98
Food	100
Retirement	102
That Is	104
Or Even Know	105
The Darker Miracle	106
Big Bill Haywood	108

III. The More Things Change, the More They Change

Simple	113
Citizens!	115
Swing	116

Ah My Country	118
Ease of the Sun	119
Martin Luther King	120
Could Be	122
In the Woods Near Cut And Shoot	124
Lick Creek	125
Like Washing the Dishes	132
Look Up,	133
Imagine	134
Again, the Brazos Valley	137
Clouds	139

Introductory Note

You may have heard of syllabic verse in which the poet writes each line to a determined number of syllables per line. I wrote this book according to a set number of words per line. Each line in a poem has the same number of words. As far as I know, no other poet has used this form. It is not a demanding one, but the choice of any form is made because the form is liberating, not constraining.

I. Place to Begin

At the Heart

Place to Begin: Bryan/College Station

An easy drive to
the sea, the land
itself slow rising hills,

the soil poor, the
dominating plants the small
post oak and red

berried yaupon, the winters
mild, the summers long,
humid, and hot, the

earth sandy clay, the
years cycling between drought
and rain, tornado free

probably, air clean, pure
strange tasting hot well
water, lakes, woods nearby

for fishing and hiking,
the police generally honest
and kind, the taxes,

the cost of living
moderate, a retreat, boring
at times, let me

be honest, we're remote
from Paris, without any
center, the town; the

epicenter for the fading
Bush family petroleum empire
that runs from Houston and

Charles Taylor

passes through Bryan/College
Station to Dallas. We
eat well, feel secure,

get left alone, and
enjoy acquaintances, yet it's
you, reader, mysterious, pleasing

as our children are, heart
of hearts singing through
wind, bringing us near

wherever be the place
whatever be the year,
even here, yes hear.

They Grow, They Go

My child, my daughter,
before school, when she
was five, I'd take
her downtown, she'd sit
in her car seat
expectant on the drive,
happy, excited, or sometimes
tired, grumpy, though often
when she said she
was not tired she'd
fall asleep, and then

we'd go there, the
place that's copyrighted and
too crass to name
in a poem (ha!)
and she'd get on
the playscape and climb
through the blue and
red plastic tubes, and
across the crosshatched netting,
and then she'd say,

"Watch me, Daddy," and
I'd look, I'd watch ,
 I'd smile, "That's great
Sweetie." I'd come over
and reach up to
where she sat and
laughed through a clear
plastic window of the
tube and say, "Daddy,
you can't get me!"

Charles Taylor

Dogmen

You think I like
the leash, the collar

to be slipped on
each morning? I do

enjoy the ambiguity here
where you don't know

if I'm speaking of
the necktie, going out

into the burning world
literally tamping the fires

down, choking them rather
to make plays down

the fallen hallways of
the worlds of power,

or could I be
taking my dog out

in the morning down
to the park with

a trusty sack to
scoop up the poop—

real of metaphorical, the
collar and leash here?

Well, how about both,
run free I shout

At the Heart

and dog gets into
the neighbor's prize roses

chasing the cat, run
free and dog gets

into territorial brawls with
sets of growlers who

bloody his side, run
free Biscuit and he

chases a squirrel in
front of a pick-up

and they both get
smashed each by a

different front tire. You
get the drift of my

drift? You think I
enjoy playing master to

slave yanking the chain
this way and that?

So let this be
my allegory of life

to embarrass us all
and give my anarchist

buddies reason to scream foul.
Who's to enjoy? We're

all dog people here
and I sing despite

Charles Taylor

the collar and leash
that love slips through,

we gather ways like
roses for touching, his

cold nose in my
hand, me scratching under

ears and neck, it's
across distances we're leaning,

across eons you can't
call paradise but we're

all dogmen, dogwomen, and
the love can move

through the hard long
miles, to bleed through.

At the Heart

Plain Song

John Woolman, he's my man,
he's the one to put

a man down on his
knees if you come from

the kind of plains that
I come from, John Woolman,

born in seventeen twenty, died
in seventeen seventy two, raised

on a Quaker farm in
what is today New Jersey—

surveyor, teacher, tailor, clerk. When
he preached those sweet words

"seasoned in Charity," he said
"to watch for the pure

opening," and I wish that
I could say every day

I watched for "the pure
opening" and worked for justice

even "toward brute creatures." So
he wore undyed rough garments

and never accepted payment for
preaching; he abstained from the

use of any product connected
with the slave trade, he

refused to travel on slave
ships, and traveled in the

noisy steerage with sailors he
saw living oppressed as slaves;

he worked to stop the
sale of rum to Indians

and worked for a just
Indian policy, he convinced farmers

to free their slaves, shipbuilders
not to sell ships to

slavers, I get on my
knees, like Dorothy Day, searching

for "the pure opening." Plain
man, man of the wooden

spoon, man who spoke from
an inner light, he's the

Christ soul I cry to
be on these bended knees.

At the Heart

Photograph of My Brother,

black and white, standing on
the Juarez bridge, at the

silver obelisk that marks the
boundary between Mexico and the

U.S. My brother's got one
leg in each country and

a wildcatter smile on his
lips like a child whose

climbed Mount Everest and feels
he's gotten away with something

he should feel guilty about
but damned if he does

I keep the picture by
the bed to remember him

and those bridges between
dreams and reality, those demon

kinds that get us strapped
to the board of unknowing,

water dripping slowly down, single
drop by single drop, onto

our foreheads like Chinese water
torture. Those failing graces I've

been told are sunk deepest
into the hope of bones,

Charles Taylor

ashes from gods who have
screwed so many brothers up,

took mine down at thirty
in powder dreams, bridge to

a god he didn't know
he sought by sweet cocaine.

Sketch of a Friend

Cal from Chicago, he
got no honorable discharge,
just a discharge neutral
and a wan handshake

for a goodbye, but
discharge rang sweet like
silver wedding bells in
his happy head as

he carried his papers
from office to office
at Fort Benning. He
got the G.I. Bill,

one hundred sixty a
month, and he fled
the country he now
hated south to Cuernavaca

where he enrolled in
an English language college,
ate beans and rice,
slept most afternoons after

class, and on weekends
wandered Mexico City streets
seeking in exile he
knew not what until

four years later he
turned twenty-eight in
nineteen seventy five and
the Vietnam War was

suddenly a rout, a
loss, so he could

return to the States
where he's now an

ultrasound tech with a
house and wife and
kids and makes sixty
thou a year but

with the Spanish he
learned ambling weekends alone
he plans to retire
to crooked Mexican city

streets to be with
a people he believes
he loves more and
finds more genuine, human.

At the Heart of the Heart

I'm looking for
a sacred place
where all sorts
of sticks can
set their killing
fires down and
slap hands together
grinning, glowing, gritty,
like the way
of the dancing
smiling Jesus who
skipped out on
his crucifixion for
the sunrise party;
imagine a spiritual
groove, a virtual
grove, in the
way the Indians
washed free the
war paint to
sit by curling
smoke and talk
with smiling hands
at the marriage
of rivers, an
intersection to end
our bleak and
bloody human traffic.

Mother Ann

She bore four children to
her husband Abraham who later
abandoned her. All four children
died in infancy. In America
she slipped into visions and

trances, became Mother Ann, the
coming second of Jesus Christ
now in female form. She
taught the judgment was near
and marriage a sin that

kept you from the Kingdom
of Heaven. Mother Ann of
the Shakers who believed that
singing and dance from Satan
shook you, opposite from the

Sufi whirling dervishes who say
their dancing brings God in.
Eighteen major communities in eight
states, the Shakers achieved. They
got attacked at times by

mobs, as the Mormons. Pacifists,
they refused to fight in
the Colonial American War. They
built simple clothes, sumptuous songs,
beautiful barns and meeting houses,

beautiful furniture too functional, spare,
elegant, believing work to be
a prayer. They adopted children.
They made converts but celibacy
remained the only way to get

At the Heart

to heaven. Four shakers survive
today in Maine. Four children
of Mother Ann's died in
infancy. Her husband Abraham deserted
when their ship reached America.

Marriage, she said, was the
devil's crooked work. Jesus, she
repeated, had never married. To
Mary Magdalene he was always
kind, yet He, always celibate.

Virge's Vigil

Arms and the man,
she sings how she
loved the hair on

his arms, how on
the right arm it
grew grey while on

the left arm still
the youthful brown as
when they first kissed,

her arms around this
man in the mortal,
the epic of love.

Parenting

After so much all
day moving and hustling
in the festive light

of all our children,
it's such a simple,
comfortable and necessary salvation,

to sit by the
window at night with
a cup of tea

listening to the branches
creaking in the old
oak and the wind

whistling around the edges
of our brick house.
The cat's asleep outside

under the pickup truck,
the dog stares in
speaking by his eyes,

Please, please, my loves.
'It's time to ramble
out around the park.'

And so I rise,
go into the night,
soon to return to

sit with you and
sip more tea, listening
to our children's dreams.

Boy in War Beirut

I admit I was dumb,
all day in the dumps,
sad and sitting with coffee

in sidewalk cafes on wide
boulevards—a notebook out,
scribbling bad surreal poetry:

"Put me in a broad
but crooked hatred, sunlight beating
crazy as the holy desert."

Now war rages that parents
know to tear their hair
about. I'm oldest, I've been

sent to purchase food though
biting sniper bullets wanting to
pounce off rigid rooftops.

I was so stupid then.
My God, now we can't
grant ourselves the pleasure of

a fast scooter to dash
about our own neighborhoods in
the dark of magic night.

I once yelled at the
sky, it's so boring here,
we need an earthquake, bad.

My mind had no manners.
I was a young man,
wild of dreams, an idiot.

Terror Infirma

I escaped
death by
raging sea

between two
Bahamian islands,
Cat Key

and Bimini
when I
was thirteen.

We were
deep inside
a cistern

it seemed,
the blue
sky a

small hole
we caught
moments above.

I lay
on the
floor of

the boat
while the
captain fought

the wheel.
I was
too sick

to think
of praying
for special

dispensation and
once on
shore I

refused to
get up
from earth

kissing over
and over
the beach

sand as
my cross.
That kept

my faith
strong till
in Japan

when I
found in
my home

the floor
and ceiling
shaking daily

in tremors
like from
an old

man's hand.
Since then
I sing

At the Heart

what I
sing from
the heart

within the
heart with
no trust

or faith
in any
one doctrine.

Futurology

Trying to write
about some technology
that will require
no footnote for
readers in the
year three thousand
I hit not
on the computer
or the shotgun,
not the stove
or the stereo
or the stethoscope
but the humble
sandal. They will
find even then
old tires to
cut and fashion
Mexican-style into
a sole fit
for any surviving
human man or
female soul, adult
or child, and
if not shoed
with old tires
then with the
cured skin of
some surviving animal
species, maybe an
evolved wilder dog
or tougher pig.
Some child will
look up at
the moon knowing
nothing of space
travel or moon
landings, tightening his

At the Heart

leather sandal straps—
and child, across
this time of
space I am
now like you,
slipping on in
this intense August,
two similar sandals.

Homesick

In Japan I'd hunger
for each new twist
or turn of my

home language, watch awful
films for novelties
of inflection, flesh notes

trilling in one word,
like "hello" when a
woman picks up a

phone picturing the face
of a lost lover
at the other end.

Hello. Hello. Hello. Hello.
Try now all the
ways to say the

word that never with
pen on page can
you come close to

capturing as did the
common mystic whirl your
two ears daily do

in the rush of
American malls that in
Japan I'd pine for.

For Akemi

I don't believe in magic much
beyond the furry buds on trees

that come in spring. I've felt
no magic beyond the dew of

the morning in the grass soaking
through my old leather hiking shoes.

But I am lighting a candle
Yes I am lighting votive candles

I'm lighting a series of candles
at the altar of my unbelief

I am lighting candles for dear Akemi
an old woman in her twenties

I m lighting this and this candle
I'm lighting more and more candles.

All through this cold Japanese house
they will launch their soft light

like Akemi's soft sharp eyes who
has been two years in hospital.

Her passions aren't my passions yet
she had passions, she loved roses

and wished to be a botanist.
So few with passions these days

Akemi has pneumonia now, her immune
system is faltering. She lived with

us six months. I knew her
gentleness, the movements of her smiles.

I am lighting for Akemi now
who is one of the gods.

When you move in passion,
you move with a muse.

The Suicides

The skill to endure,
you feel for those
born without this simple

mother's milk and habit.
I watched one evening
an elderly homeless man

climb in a bush
at the park for
a poor night's sleep.

What curse brought others
to this green and
dying planet to then

ignore the meal of
spring, to have no
bones for going on?

Some whispering of evil
leaves in the mind?
I want to know

to begin a blessing
for a friend who
is folding up in

grief and pain; blessings
for him and for
his son suddenly gone

who we never dreamed
was troubled, never guessed
found this sold world

Charles Taylor

a burden more than
we found the world
a burden, meant much

more when he said—
as we all have said—
I can't go on.

No Ambition

I have a father
to thank for no
ambition—a father,

bless him, whose eyes
drooped sorrow and suffering
to compose a kindness—

yet who drank at
the dinner family table
and cursed ferociously those

who'd moved ahead of
him, never for talent
but because of class

and money and prestige
schools, and I loved
my father, and I

believed him as I
love now and believe
this April afternoon, though

father's long been underground,
rests unambitious I hope,
peaceful in his coffin.

Charles Taylor

Be Here Never
   with thanks to T.S. Eliot's *Four
   Quartets* and to Ram Dass

Time past and time
future are contained in
time now and time

future and time present
are contained in time
past and be here

now and be here
then and be here
tomorrow—then take a

break my friend, take
off for a while
and be here never.

Miracles

Jesus may never again
walk on the water
but would you look

at those alligators, the
way they blend in
with the muddy water

the way swishing their
tails they so silently
slide through the wet.

Charles Taylor

Marx, Brother?

Sure I'm a Marxist,
always have been, always
will be, he told

the dentist looking for
commies under every tooth.
Our five-year program

remains to get ourselves
some decent harps and
shoot grapefruits by pulling

back on harp strings—
say the secret weapon
you win five hundred

dollars, *Das Kapital* or
hey! Do you want
to buy a duck?

Words are 4

Take a month off,
get that albatross off
your frail neck like
the guru Coleridge says

and in case you
don't know what an
albatross is, let me
add, it's a bird

of the sea, long
winged white with black
feather tips, symbolically a
source of frustration or

guilt. So anyway, take
a month off from
the word love, don't
say or even whisper

the old word to
anyone, not even to
your favorite flavored ice
cream, take the month

off and let that
foul bird fly off
your neck because now
you're going to do

love each hopeful moment
the word slips up
to the circle of
your lips, you'll do

a kiss, a caress,
you'll go wash the
dishes, make the beds,
you could get that

old Clue game out
of the closet and
sit down all together
around the table, I'm

singing that the way
to be is to do
for a while, and you'll
love it, I'm telling

you, I helped a
gal who was my
enemy, she and her
husband sought by subtle

arias to take my
life's work from me.
All I did was be
a chauvinist, help her

move heavy audio-visual
equipment from one classroom
to another. For a
moment, it was love.

Excuses

I miss you, Kathy,
I miss our long
telephone calls where you
made me self-conscious,
saying, Your wife is
not going to like
all our long discussions.

It was always business,
it was always the
politics going on *ad
nausea* up at work.
Sometimes you told me
things I wasn't sure
to believe, how you'd

missed two days of
work when your former
Oxford professor husband was
discovered overdosed in a
derelict motel; he'd come
home one day and
said no God existed,

so everything was permitted.
Was he reading Dostoyevsky?
I had asked. You
said that though you
loved him you had
to get your daughter
out of there, he'd

quit his teaching, lay
around the house, drank
and did drugs. The
Japanese are mostly atheists,
I say, yet they never
steal. Kathy, you died
so suddenly. One day

they took out a
small lump and you
said it was OK. The
next you were gone.
Kathy, I wasn't much
of a friend. I'd
loaned you many books

you promised to return
but never did. I
gave you my short
novel manuscript to read
and you never responded.
We had you over
for dinner but you

never reciprocated. I am
shit. I haven't learned
a thing about the
simple art of forgiveness,
or how to care
when a friend's in
need. With love it

seems we just don't
know what to do.
I don't think I
got good lessons from
my parents. See what
a fuck I am, making
excuses. I promise, if

a time comes when
strangers or friends are
dying, I will be
up on the bed
with them, if they
so wish, my arms
wrapped around, hugging, kissing.

So It Goes

Mother, your mother died
at your birth, you
never talked of it,

you were always unhappy
and almost always angry,
cursing the Jews and

the Catholics and the
Negroes, mother, your mother
died at your birth,

you stayed in your
room for most of
my childhood smoking cigarettes.

Mother, I remember you
always said vote your
self-interest, the world's

not fair, and never,
never, ever feel guilty
for what you've done.

I'll give you this,
mother, you knew how
to avoid work, use

men, and you lived
long, mother whose mother
died at your birth,

for you worked my
father hard, though finally
after the cement of

silences all those years
where no one spoke
of what was going

on, after your second
suicide attempt and five
years of sleeping in

two different rooms, mother
whose mother died when
you were born, father

gave up the game
and shipped you away
to a nursing home

where for thirty years
we came to visit
as you lived alone

and made no friends
and died watching a
basketball game on TV.

At the Heart

Lies of History

"Guys, get this," I say
to my high school buddies.
"We're not far from where
we played sandlot ball and

not far from where she's
buried, Red Emma I'm talking
about. There's an Emma Goldman
Clinic in Iowa City where

I practice law. Emma went
to jail in nineteen seventeen
for giving speeches and passing
out birth control pamphlets on

the streets. My cousin John
went to jail for knocking
up a seventeen year old
girl in nineteen fifty-eight

when rubbers were the only
available birth control. Can you
imagine? Emma was the first
to defend in public the

rights of gays. She was
a diva, spoke to huge
crowds, till Hoover declared her
the most dangerous woman in

America and deported her to
her native Russia where in
nineteen twenty three she conceived
My Disillusionment with Russia, showing

up those power hungry Bolsheviks.
There's a Red Emma's Bookstore
and Coffee House in Philadelphia,
and here's her grave near

the Haymarket Labor heroes yeah,
I know you want to
play golf on this stupendous
day, my reunion suburban classmates,

but it's my car. Look
at the monument, think what
is it *now* that they
don't want us to know."

This Child
for my daughter Lisa

can't be my blood,
my blood does not
have such hypnotic eyes,

my blood walks on
different streets and sings
songs with less sunlight

and more shadow, mine
has dreams to never
hold a child so

tenderly, my blood was
always looking away and
headed for the door.

American
for Takako

I learned to love
you before I knew
the who of you

you really are, and
can't turn off that
spigot though I don't

share your need for
money or status or
power. I try not

to laugh or show
contempt. I know you
are from a land

that suffered war, poverty,
occupation. I've had a
way too easy way,

but all I can
gather myself to say
is, daily, I make

the effort and the
sparks that fly are
a fire I love.

Ancestor

It feels right, knowing
exactly where your shit
goes, knowing you have

dug your own hole
and you have put
it there, not putting

your shit on another
helpless as a child.
It's like chopping off

the heads of your
own chickens if you
are in that soup.

So simple, to walk
deep into the woods
and dig your hole,

unbuckle and drop your
trousers in a stance
like the way women

out in the waving fields
once squatted down to
the task of birth.

Charles Taylor

I feel a better

person having now installed
a water heater, they're
heavy beasts and you
wrestle them like bears
into the right position
for hooking up the
pipes, getting the tank
up inside the drip
pan, then hammering the
shims in to make
the tank level. My
water heater doesn't run
on sunlight, I'm sad
to say to former
Senator Gore, it runs
on natural gas and
I had to wrap
the threads from the
gas pipe with silicon
tape, and paint the
plastic pipe with glue
from a tube. I'm
not sure we need
a water heater; bathing
cold could be more
holy, healthy, challenging, bracing,
but I live with
women who like it
hot and have been
making growling noises day
and night that they
might decamp for better
digs than poor mine.

Home

All my life
like a haunting
this tale

told to us
by our mother—
that the house

where we then
lived had been
a small forest

in the city,
and that the
woods had been

bulldozed in the
spring when the
birds sat nesting.

"You should have
seen the broken
small eggs, my

mother said. "You
should have seen
all the bodies

of the hairless
baby birds, I've
never felt right

about this place,
after such massacre,"
my mother claimed,

Charles Taylor

though she fought
and shouted when
my father talked

of moving to
another state for
a better job.

Dear Reader

These stores I tell,
maybe you've heard them
all before. Maybe not.

You see it's simple,
I'm lonely and want
to hold you here,

feeling I'm alive as
long as our soft
lips are almost touching.

Charles Taylor

On the Assassinations of JFK, RFK, Martin Luther King, and Malcolm X

Sure we were sad
all the time mad

Sure I acted bad
played being the cad

but it was all
we had for those

deranged days when they
were killing almost everybody.

we were swallowing karate
chops to the heart

and we had to
keep going somehow through

the war body counts,
sure I was deep

down mad I painted
flowers on my car

wanting to pull out
someone's hair, break windows,

slug a pig in
the face, it was

like a mantra when
I heard it on

the news, nothing was
left inside to cry

At the Heart

or care, inside was
crushed skulls, the smell

of dead crows, they
were taking them all,

it was night and
it would always be

night, but I went
ahead with the words,

how they can hold
when they're slippery, softer

than feathers yet can
move freight trains through,

even send soft blessings
into a howling night.

Oneida

You think of silverware
when you see the
word *Oneida* but between
eighteen forty eight and

eighteen sixty eight there
were two hundred and
fifty-eight adults in
a community in upstate

New York who succeeded
in crafts and farming,
had their own schools,
churches and hospitals, and

in governance and in
daily life created near
equality between women and
men, believing humans without

original sin, regenerated pure
in Jesus Christ. They
practiced complex marriage, married
all to each other.

It didn't last long
beyond the time the
leadership passed from father
to dictatorial son, who

was agnostic. The setup
wasn't simple, but don't
you love them, these
crackpots, these risk takers?

At the Heart

I celebrate crazy Christian
groups from the past,
Radical dressed and seeking
a more perfect union.

One Answer

Took sleeping pills for
two years and always
I'd build up immunity,

return to the natural
state of insomnia where
you reach a condition

of 'I don't care'
that can be Buddhist
detachment from things or

depression. I tried a
lot of brands of
different pills but none

worked for long. Then
I learned, on closing
my eyes, to whisper

'Thank you' three times,
and now my sleep
is not perfect but

dreams are more interesting
and I sleep through
much of the night

to wake not rested
but trusting to the
pleasurable flavors of possibility,

to that kind of
day whose innumerable blooms
I need not control.

In Time

Exhaustion brings its truth;
you no longer long
romantically, no longer long

for it all whatever
all it is but
sit and sip tea

blessed by the dim
of your room and
your loose fitting pajamas.

Charles Taylor

The Stranger, The Reader

There are but these
few unforgotten fragments of
phrases I carry here

and dare compare to
red roses held behind
the back and then

given to pairs of
eyes I've never met
but wish to stay:

around us all, broad
sky and silence, so
I say we must

say the phrases that
tie with pliable thread
our lonely hearts together.

At the Heart
So Much

Killing there is, as you
no doubt know, going on

as we speak, one to
another, by our lips engaged,

and a sorrow that runs
right through our bones because

we can not rise from
our labors and go out

into the now quiet fields
at least where the blood

has run and the flies
do buzz to offer prayers

and dig graves with a
shovel, for killing, *en masse*,

that is, going on right
as I write, yet yesterday

I sat waiting for my
cell phone to ring, my

daughter to call because she's
concerned about the drugs they

sell on the school bus
and the sex going on

in the back in what
should carry her safely home

Charles Taylor

from her tree shaded high
school, so it's everywhere, I

guess, darkness that blights the
light at the heart of

the heart, that we must
learn when to fight and

when to draw back to
avoid a fight and keep

a hope for tenderness,
to hold on to sanity .

Keep It Easy
For Takako

You're for me
I'm for you
so the love

lovely goes, growing
latterly up and
down. We are

roots, we are
leaves, the stem,
we make seeds,

climb stairs up,
sit on stoops
to catch rest.

Yes that's the
way it goes,
in the shining

tree inside the
moment, not straying
from the simple

heart at the
heart of the
heart of things.

Moment

Here you are
reading paper words
looking for life

You look up
and a green
gecko with an

obsidian eye sits
scrunched between these
two blades of

our Venetian blinds
that let the
morning sun inside

streaming across the
kitchen table to
where you write

Still, as in
still, the now
and the now.

At the Heart

Conundrum

Colin Wilson gave
up his flat,

got rid of
his job to

make the rent,
slept in a

sleeping bag under
a park tree

close to the
British Museum to

gain time to
do the research

to write his
book on being

The Outsider that
he thought through

carefully so that
he wouldn't become

one, got married
and raised kids,

wrote other books
not out of

passion but a
need for money.

Charles Taylor

They're forgotten, I'm
sorry to say,

nearly everyone's not
reading, but grandchildren!

Albert Schweitzer

"If I save an insect from a puddle, life has devoted itself to life, and the division of life against itself has ended."

The Jain saints
sweep the ground
with peacock feathers

that have fallen
from a peacock
naturally so that

they can hopefully
avoid stepping on
and killing any

insects in the
soil; they walk
naked through India's

back roads eating
fruit the villagers
gather for them

fallen from trees.
Alexander turned his
armies toward home,

gave up his
dream to conquer
all of Asia,

it is said,
after an encounter
with Jain saints.

A Day

I climbed past
fall after fall
in Japan once

high through the
mist of mountains
on a rare

morning when I
was still by
water crashing, at

peace with this
notorious world, free
of its desires

Yes in Japan
I climbed in
peace on a

twisty, tricky, rocky
path up beyond
fall after fall,

pure and thundering,
yet through the
tall green trees,

the pure blue
sky up high,
calm and cloudless.

To See Anew

The park was
huge and full
of secret hollows

where we four
might have communed
with the inner

light or the
outer blessings in
a joyous solitude,

but my Japanese
friends, tribal, social,
sweet and polite,

they led me
to the circle
where everyone sat

together sharing what
they brought—stories
and questions, rice

balls, cool barley
tea, and crunchy
dicon yellow pickles.

Tsukmimi

Take a plastic
tarp behind Tokyo's
grand Ueno Station

on a night
of the full
moon. Just once

in your life
stay up all
night drinking sake

under the fresh
cherry blossoms and
grow sad singing

songs to your
hometown and life
as a child.

You will be
all right sucking
the gentle light

of our mother
moon's lambent milk
of utter delight.

Key

He's an old man,
my self, who quickly

begins to puff climbing
the steep temple stairs

at Narita Shrine, an
old man who has

a secret love always
for the sibilance of

sweet water over stones,
an old man who

knows to get lost
in deep woods or

on a thin path
up a mountain, an

old man who knows
that true paradise is

by time acquired, at
the heart of your

heart, my friends, in
your own good nature.

Memo to Sensei
For Takako

This document is both technical
and poetic. You should know
that your lips are more
supple than the wings of
cranes in flight, and the
way your shoulders shift when
you walk makes me weak
all week. It compares with
the shoulder strokes Michelangelo made
in the Sistine Chapel painting
on his back. I hope
you'll grant me some poetic
license and not report this
memo to superiors at this
language school. Everything is moving
smoothly along—as smooth as
your skin—with my accent
and vocabulary. I will sign
the contract for your private
instruction for a year, and
you will sign, with hands
as lovely as mountain springs.
Shall we say at three thirty,
this Friday, June 14th?
Sensei, always my deepest regards,
your humble and bumbling American.

II. The River Runs

On Learning the "to be" Verb has been Banned from School Essays

She is a laid
back verb, is is,
but is is here
to stay, no to
be or not to
be when it comes
to is, is was
and is will be,
is has been and
has not hasn't been;
is do so is
be so for is,
is what it is.

Death Dream

He touched me on
the shoulder chiding me

for having in my
freezer way too much

Neapolitan ice cream. Poor
insomniac death, haunted by

the many frozen faces
of those he'd handed

the black poker chip.
He came in my

room and switched on
the TV, setting the

sound low for background
company. My cats were

growling from outside. "Come
on cats," he groused,

"you know I'm just
the sign board man

for the boss above."
Death left on the

wind of an owl
hooting, shot out before

the first slim rays
of sol. He hid

At the Heart

in the glove box
of my antique red

Studebaker, polished and ready
for a better parade,

the poet's light being
too dim for him.

August Morning

Before our century
I don't believe
many got to
explore many jolly
pleasures. People went
to church or
to laboring in
the fields and
later to assembly
lines in places
like textile mills.
I'm doing nothing
now but listening
to the long
drawn crack of
thunder and watching
a hard slant
of fierce rain,
peering through a
crack in the
blinds from where
it's dry, comfortable.
I haven't spit
at work for
over a month
and still the
larder is full.
Did you know
that thunder sounds
exactly like dropping
corrugated sheets of
steel used in
constructing those cheap
ugly steel buildings?
The rolling of
the next batch
of thunder sounds

At the Heart

like the firing
of ominous guns
and I think
of a small
boy in one
hundred and twenty
degree Iraq, he
could be dying
now collaterally in
the defense of
our freedom, it's
Saturday and soon
after the rain
blows on through
the shoppers will
be up heading
for the mall,
to make, in
freedom, their perfectly
returnable purchasing decisions.

1949, Oregon

My grandmother when
I was six
took me outside
and taught me
how to cut
kindling, I'd do
it in the
morning early when
she made pancakes
and in the
afternoon for soup
and the evenings
when she fried
potatoes and meat,
my small hands
standing the boards
up on end
letting it go
to get fingers
out of the
way and striking
with the hatchet
on the top
edge to split
the wood before
it tumbled down.
I brought in
the kindling in
a basket, opened
up the cast
iron stove and
tossed the kindling
into the orange
heat. My grandma
never said one
word but by
her way I

At the Heart

learned and I
knew her loving
heart, that she
found the ways
of her world
good and beautiful.

Punishment

My father, a doctor,
smart, a man of

many gifts, had sad
eyes and a skill

at spanking. Ask me.
Ask my sister. He

was a gentle man
and his whacks were

never whips of anger,
never slashes of the

mean. The game was
mostly the setup. He

sent us in the
bathroom to think about

what we had done.
I pondered and am

proud to say I
never made excuses or

tried to weasel out.
I lay across his

lap butt naked; more
discretion was given to

my sister. Dad sat
on the toilet seat.

At the Heart

I recall one month
in summer he'd told

me to leave our
beagle puppy alone—but

out of curiosity and
not any real meanness—

I hit her on
the head with a

hammer. One autumn he'd
said to stay out

of the cask of
roofing tar he stored

in the garage. It
took a day to scrub

the black off with
turpentine. Mom had said

to watch the India
ink and I spilt it

all over her Turkish
carpet. I don't recall

what more graceful sins
caught my younger sister.

Three times my bare
soft skin met the

cold hard hairbrush, three
unforgotten times in a

Charles Taylor

childhood where I speak
mostly of my father's

grey-blue eyes of
sorrow that came from

I know not where,
and of his gentleness.

Song for the Buddha, Bubba

Get me out of
Buddha, get me August

heat on a beatific
baseball diamond inching off

first trying to steal
second. Get me out

of sky empty mind,
get me in bed

in a sorry small
town with the blond

bartender I've joked with
for years over beers.

Get me far away
from four noble truths,

put 'em in a black
trash bag at the

curb. I got clam
chowder on the stove.

You want to cut
up some leeks? I

came here to trim
my nails, I came

to re-roof my house,
I came here to

find special lenses like
Joseph Smith and believe

I could read sacred
texts written on lost

gold tablets in forgotten
foreign tongues, way too

heavy for four strapping
lads to carry down

some New York state
mini-mountain. Don't forget

salvation is always looming
in cheap wristwatches. Someone

get the enlightened one
the Double Bubble and

teach him the holiness
of chewing gum, how

to slow blow bubbles
big as your head.

The Blind Man

"It was on
the Interstate," Ricardo
tells me. "The

freeway between Albuquerque
and Santa Fe,
where the road

runs between mountain
ranges flat and
straight. Hadley had

never driven and
I was just
out of prison,

into a new
wisdom. Life was
precious but freedom

made me seek
new ways to
be reckless, so

I pulled off
on the shoulder
and walked Hadley

around and that
blind old man,
he started driving,

slowly bringing up
speed to fifty-five,
the limit at

the time he
didn't want to
break. 'A little

to the left,
a little to
the right,' I'd

say, now and
then, but mostly
Hadley did it

by the pressure
of the wind
on the front

windshield. Angels worked
in his heart.
He was the

wisest man I
knew, with an
instinct that spoke

out of his
poet's third eye,
frisky and risky."

Love
for Takako

We haven't talked
of it lately,
how we may
not even be
in the same
room but I'll
know how you
feel, if I
feel like you
feel—and sometimes
our feelings get
mixed, we don't
know where they
started or who
feels what, it's
not maddening and
not magical, what
do you think,
would you agree,
this thing between
us that does
go on happening?

Sister God

She lies under a tree,
she lies under a blue
umbrella waving secret hands at
the bright inconstant stars, she
lies by the broken ruins
of Michelangelo's David and she
lies on the banks of
smoky rivers I will never
see or smell to know.
She rises and steps over
a sun that's never angry,
she rises and walks into
the mercury of bright irises,
she crosses to the oasis
and blesses the tents that
are gathered to gather the
songs of the sandy springs,
she crosses footbridges to villages
where they have her name
and she speaks their languages,
I have no idea what
she means alone in the
box of my gender yet
find I am drawn to
honor her way by service.

Taking on the Big One

A while it's been
since I opened the
tackle box and tried
to tackle the big

one, the great white
blob out in life's
ocean, Mister Death, with
his swell bloodhound nose

that smells his upcoming
meals miles away. I
usually like to picture
death as a shrouded

stranger hidden behind the
curtains, the toes of
scruffy shoes sticking out,
a passive sort of

guy waiting for the
simmer down before slipping
out and waving down
a taxi for the

next town. Truth is
death's rather an anachronism
as envisioned, a quaint
return to a time

when we were certain
all sorts of spirits
haunted the woods or
hid in the basement.

The term *personification* just
about deconstructed you Mister
Death, labeled you an
abstraction given human qualities.

Precisely speaking a shark
is no personification, it
being an animal, not
a person, but the

spate of improvised deaths
we see today behind
auto wheels right here
at home or overseas

in warring nations, well,
I'd say today death's
a shark that motors
well all our seas.

King Debs

died in Lindlahr nature cure
Sanitarium in my suburban hometown
of Elmhurst, Illinois in nineteen
twenty-six at the age

of seventy. King Debs was
never mentioned in my years
of school in Elmhurst from
the forties to the sixties,

though he was nominated for
the Nobel Peace Prize and
received six percent of the
vote when running for president.

Good old forgotten Debs was
in and out of prison
for his union organizing
and political activism. He wrote,

"Your Honor, years ago I
recognized my kinship with all
living beings, and I made
up my mind that I

was not one bit better
than the meanest on earth."
I bring his words to
you, reader, for I know

that inside this moment, you
yearn to keep it simple,
and in the heart of
your heart, if you can

Charles Taylor

strip down and kick away
all those rubble walls of
heavy ideologies, you too know,
in your heart of hearts.

The Coming

If you've walked in your
heavy galoshes into a farmer's
wheat field covered with fresh
snow on a bright Sunday
morning, if you have listened
with a sharp delight to
the snap of frozen wheat
stems under your feet mixed
with the crunch of snow,
well now my family, what
more can anyone say about
the coming kingdom of God?

You Get It

I know there's
more than these

words, know that
the space around

the words is
the wiser grace.

I know there's
more than your

lips up curved,
more than the

hazel of eyes,
know that it's

the space between
what's seen and

unseen that I
call every morning,

the unknown of
your tenuous roses.

Odd Attitude

What is the sound
of one hand clapping,
the sound of cumulous
clouds meeting snowy mountains

the sound of sounds
refusing offers to negotiate,
the sound of gum
removing its wrapper, the

sound of knuckles knocking
on cotton candy, the
sound of trees falling
on foam rubber, the

sound of bacon frying
in a vacuum, the
sound of Zen strangled
by piano wire; I've

been doing nothing, nothing—
am the sound of
pie, already eaten, thrown
by a happy man.

Brazos Valley

lines that go lopping
along with no transcendent
leaps, no snaps of
the whip, lines that
meander in light and
shadow down a path
in the woods; winds
slight through the trees
by the river, a
dog barking in the
distance, and birds chirping,
the underbrush obscuring so
you can't see but
the melody feeds and
tells you they're up
in the trees. I've
grown comfortable, in love
with this land of
small trees and heavy
underbrush, I don't feel
claustrophobic anymore in these
new truths, I don't
feel that I'm lost.

Word Play, Make Way

I want a beaver
moon, I want a
strontium ninety moon and
not just any moon
but a balloon moon
for the buck and
a swan moon that
sings for the donut
maker and the night
dishwasher and an armadillo
moon to dance with
the gibbous moon and
then the lonely moon
that jumps over the
Chinese lantern mountain with
the cow to slip
away with the spoon
on a rainy June—
now who's the bride
now who's the groom,
whose going to swoon
when we're in tune,
knowing moon's no goon
but wizened a rune.

Charles Taylor

Fundamental

Fat squirrel sleeping
in a nook
of a tree
limb while I
watch out the
window washing dishes,
this poem, divine,
knows we two
are divine, too.

Auto Elegy

Sometimes I think
the only thing
that makes sense
is to be
on the road

how I love
the stereoscopic view,
the majesty of
moving through all,
remaining so free

and disconnected. I
prefer a hound
by my side
or with her
nose out the

window. I like
the sitting in
solitude or in
the swing of
music from the

radio. No obligato.
Keep your eye
out, steer clear
of cops or
fence jumping deer.

What god did
the old monks
speak of but
the same god,
the good god

of the two
lane blacktop, sights
splaying colorfully by,
clouds steady shifting
overhead, glory road:

6/2/11
gasoline: $3.75/gallon.

Transvestite

His long hair and
beard died purple, this

pure Christ, standing on
the corner of Fifth

and Congress in downtown
Austin, in a skin

tight leopard skin dress
that ends above the

knee. What drives him
to this busy intersection

for such display, what
hungry wolf of soul

makes these demands I
know but have no

way of knowing. Still,
the hungry wolf of

my soul signals assent
to his pure courage.

Man Alone on His Porch

You there about to explode
sitting clenching a can of
cold beer, I across the

street gaily walking my dog,
my frisky and healthy golden
retriever, your hate reaches me,

I feel your anger, I
am a stranger here, though
once I lived in this

West Texas town, you alone
there after work in the
June heat and late sun,

I try not to provoke you,
take hidden glances trying to
intuit just how I could

have transgressed your line of
sight, your territory, with my
easy jauntiness, while you have

sweated a job you hate
all day in a needed
hell not of your own

making. I am white and
you are brown and I
keep my dog to the

cracked sidewalk not wanting any
incident to interfere with my
further trip out West. Can

At the Heart

you see inside to the
place that holds my hatred
of this town I risked

all to escape twenty years
ago? My anger has nothing
to do with your anger

but my anger could meet
your anger and with this
big dog at my side

who's to say who would
win if you can't contain
yourself and dash across the

road to relieve your pain
that has its justice but
is fueled by crazed loneliness

which sets a mind to
wandering down far unknown arroyos
unchecked by loving hands. No

way for you to know
the rage that lives within
my heart, the suffering endured

that makes us brothers who,
in a better world, might,
in the late light of

this empty street, find good
words in common and meet
instead in a man's embrace.

Food

The frogs got it wrong,
the round heads had it
right, if it tastes good
then you know it's not

good for you, food's to
be painful, like chopping wood
or chomping on Grape Nuts,
food is labor, labor is

life, you should feel you've
climbed a mountain on the
straight and narrow by the
end of your eating journey,

food is character building, strengthens
your morals, keeping the cholesterol
down, the arteries clean, not
dirty clogged pipes, ah that

nutritious brown rice that humps
in the belly like a
nest of acorns, praise be
to raw carrots and blah

tofu, stewed yams and purple
peppered cabbage. No chocolates, no
pies, no whipped mélanges, no
cakes, crepes or creams, no

moon pies, no biscuits and
gravy, chicken fried steak or
bacon. When you eat you're
sleeping on a plank, a

At the Heart

thin sheet to keep you
warm. You rise in the
dark at five for chapel
and five miles of jogging;

you're lean and mean and
rumored to have a bitter
temper, to hate music and
despise all pets, to own

a butt so skinny that
sitting on chairs is painful
yet it's claimed you live
cozy and consecrated by God.

Retirement

My friend, he's gone
to high mountain Mexico,
south of Monterey, an

old silver mining town,
isolated, somewhat falling down.
Last time I was

there Germans were trying
to open an art
gallery and children searched

through the trash we
threw out, sleeping in
the high cold of

tents. All night I
heard the tinkling of
goat bells, and I'd

say a side of
all of us is
called this way, to

the ascetic isolation, the
quiet long distances and
the sweet pain of

loneliness, but I long
to nurture a few.
I see agony in

eyes that require an
elder touch with words
that only elders know

At the Heart

how to light in
the dark of loss
or pain; this is

what I need and
what I will do
in what years remain—

help make the light
light up, however small,
in hungry lost souls.

That is

I yearn to rid
myself of the wood
of arrows that poke
hard words into the
target of the page,
make discreet particles framed
by the emptiness of
silent white—yet blessed
we come with eyes
to blur the space
between our imperfect words
that are but signs
of sounds that river-
move in what lives
flowing like stars, like
turning earth, like expanding
space. We're given to
know that what we
are has no form,
lives by its flowing.

Or Even Know

He's at the shelter downtown
where the Bryan homeless stay,
he's back from the Iraq
War and he's lost a
leg and he doesn't know
if he can find work,
if he can make it
in this town away from
friends and home but he's
heard the local economy's good

No luck so far and
his money's running out. Tonight
he's been placed on a
suicide watch. They worry because
of the things he's been
through and what he's been
saying, how he made the
sacrifice but these our local
assholes, they don't seem
to care, or even know.

A Darker Miracle

Something's happened to
my brother she
said in the
morning when we
climbed out of
the marriage bed

It's just a
dream, I said,
as we both
headed to the
kitchen to fry
the kids eggs.

The phone rang
on the wall
and she answered
in her frayed,
flowered flannel pajamas
holding the eggs.

She was silent
a long time,
just nodding her
head, and then
she turned to
me and said

"It's Michael from
Oklahoma City. He
says my brother
at some party
came up behind
a man and

At the Heart

shot him in
the back of
the head. I'll
need to catch
the bus up
to help out."

She started to
cry and said
she loved her
brother and needed
to go do
what needed doing.

Charles Taylor

Big Bill Haywood (1869-1928)

ONE BIG UNION,
that was Big
Bill Haywood's dream

ONE BIG UNION
for all workers
whatever their skills

whatever their race
or their creed,
Haywood hewed to

the simple: one
big union international
to fight for

the poor and
the hungry, the
damaged and misused,

for fair wages
and fair treatment
in the hard

work of factories
and fields, ONE
BIG UNION, everywhere

in Johannesburg, Ulan
Bator, Beijing, Hamburg,
Chicago, can you

imagine if he'd
gotten fair treatment
before the law

At the Heart

where our dying
world might be
instead—flowers festooning!

III. The More Things Change, the More They Change

Simple

The light trash in
this low pollution town
allows a man to
catch a few stars
on a cloudless night,
and tonight, March night,
big moon high as
I walk trails through
a large spot of
woods, a spotlight moon,
making shadows from my
body on the wet
ground, and the trees,
the trees, it's as
if they've been painted
with a coat of
silver. In March the
leaves aren't full out,
so moonlight can penetrate
and paint the ground
all around in moving
shadows and milky silver
as if the world
were held inside a
fine silver tone print
by Ansell Adams, photographer.
I call my son on
the cell and say
get out in the
yard, you've got to
see this blinding moon,
musician, look at her
face, squint your eyes,
and then you've got
to walk around in
the silver, coinage of
another realm, grandpa would

say the fairy realm,
given to be seen
once or twice a
life, so to muse
the calm of such
divine down into the
haunted hollow human heart.

Citizens!

*For Captain C. Bruce Taylor, volunteer,
US Army Air Force, World War II*

I wish we could love these men
in their bodies, soldiers I mean,
and the women too—not the
bar bulging types of the suburban
gyms, steroid tempted but the lean
ones, close cropped hair, long veins
gorgeous vines running up and down
powerful and loving arms, I wish we
could love these mostly out of
our small impoverished places, humble,
claptrap or adobe homes, love them
even when they go on their
drunken painful rages and almost burn
down their neighbor's woods, love them
in their loss of legs, their
jaws blown away, love them in
their coffins draped with flags soon
folded away, I wish we would
love them as we know the
love of muscle, the love of
bodies, the beauty of the unit,
brothers, sisters marching together, we know
that love, we've been on baseball
teams, we've loved our own limbs,
and we know we are in
the great tree of limb to limb,
I wish we could love them,
I wish we could care enough
to be more careful with how
we spend their lives, out of
a sorrow and deep heart, for
we do need these men and
these women, we need their muscled
pride and their courage, for the
predators hiding at the edge of
fields, luring always in the night.

Swing

Your heart, does it dangle
inside your chest like a
pendulum inside a large clock?

Do you feel its sway
between the furthest reaches on
its ribby arc, between joy

that holds a moment and
then the rush down that's
its own kind of rush,

to its opposite, what do
we call it, sorrow or
grief?—all the while you

are turning as the earth
is turning so that each
ascent and descent is different,

each joy, each sorrow, each
balance, even when the pendulum
points down, has its difference,

its own character. Do you
want these swings to go
away? Do you want to

end the slow and dizzy
rush, to move to stillness,
to silence? What do you

wish for? It comes, does
it not? Glimpses from the
heart's third eye, such glimpses

At the Heart

of gold, gifts to reach
"for the pure opening," the
breath within the breath, that

which in words has no
name, but we are made
of blood, hungry animals too

howling for the moon. Our
pump's a pendulum made to
swing, brother, sister, made for

music with moments of harmony,
then a crying out of
tune, then sad like Tchaikovsky,

disconsolate the madness riding inside
the melody, and at last,
the heart swinging to rise

to its own sky, to
the arc of song beyond
song, the heart of joy.

Ah My Country,

Would we were
kind, kind as
the rattlesnakes, they
go fleeing first,
they don't want
trouble, twisting like
river water away—
then if trouble
continues they rattle
their built in
snare drums. Would
we were kind
as their kind,
not marching to
drums but trying
to ward off
battle, willing to
run and rattle,
not getting all
poofed up, first
out with the
poison flashing fangs.

At the Heart

Ease of the Sun

Daughter's school supplies to buy
this last summer's day, and

my mother says to call
to get her hair done

on Friday next, and the
car I've got to pull

the plug, drain and change
the oil, necessaries to love

these weeks, this life, to
move in a modest way

in the pleasure, power,
the ease of the sun.

Charles Taylor

Martin Luther King

It was in that voice,
you can get a sense
of it listening to recordings.

It was in his voice—
a wavering, a deep sense
of heart that wrung all

hearts in the same aria
of soulful suffering and joy.
The timbre of that voice,

a sound that carried his
soul, a soul of such
depth that the deep good

buried in the forgotten places
of our hearts rose up.
I'll tell you one story,

one tale that I believe
can bring back to all
what is in us like

that voice that so lifted
the air setting us afire
with hope of change. You

know Selma, you know the
Washington march and what he
said of the dream, but

the story I have to
tell is when he was
a child, when he was

At the Heart

playing with his brother Alfred
downstairs in their home, and
Alfred slid down the banister

and accidentally knocked his grandma
down. She lay on the
floor without moving and Martin

grew distraught as he stood
immobilized thinking his dear "Mama"
dead and then the boy

ran upstairs and threw himself
out the window, falling twelve
feet, laying motionless as his

family called his name. Both
were bruised but fine. Martin
grew up to give us

the dream and the redemptive
hope, that care still singing
in our sometimes wavering hearts.

All one needs is to
heed his words, listen to
the timbre of his voice.

Charles Taylor

Could Be
   for Connie Williams

I don't know, Dear Reader,
why you should concern yourself

over my conceits but thanks
for kindly coming on board.

Can I tell you, friend,
of old affections lost and

found again out in far
West Texas, in remote small

cities full of the bright
waving light of mesquite trees.

One does enjoy driving through
the neighborhoods off the main

highway where the grass never
grows well to see what

people have done with their
yards, to see the century

plants planted, the great rocks
hauled in and arranged in

the yard, chairs set out
around a table made from

a giant spool left behind
by the telephone company when

done stringing lines, why you'll
see gorgeous old cars rusting

At the Heart

back to earth, old rusted
plows, you'll see aquamarine painted

concrete statuary of Jesus and
Mary, you'll see bottle trees,

giant logs of driftwood hauled
in all the way from

the sea—things found or
made by folks not afraid

to be what they, the
land, and who they claim

for a God who loves
them, wishes they could be.

In the Woods near Cut And Shoot

You brought her off the road
and laid her on the kitchen
table—road kill, gorgeous, her pelt
clean, vigorous, youthful. Under the kitchen
fluorescent she seemed full of moonlight.
The forest ranger came and examined
her teeth, her limbs and nails.
We stood silent, respectful. James
wished to know if she was pure
blood, or if her genes were
partly-dog. She seemed all wolf
to me and to the forest
ranger, who carried her off for
refrigeration. All I knew was she
was lean and in her prime.
I felt her belly to see if
she might be pregnant. I wanted
so to believe the pine trees
around us wept a silent mourning.

Lick Creek
For Jimmie Killingsworth

Park the pickup at the old pump jack,
then down the paved road to the equestran
entrance, I climb over the wooden fence, the
dog shimmies under, and we amble a mucky

tall grass trail down to where the archery
range used to be before the archers unstrung
their dreams—though once I found, floundering deep
in the woods off trail, one of their

silver shafts stuck in the ground (it's now
lost somewhere in the garage). My dog tracks
ten years wise, got him in nineteen ninety-
eight and brought him here on the second

day, he was a large puppy, but nervous
away from his kin; he kept his eyes
on me while excitedly sniffing down the crooked
trails up and down the steep ravines a

bit spooked by the spinning moan of racecars
from the Texas World Speedway six miles away.
We've been out here at least once a
week since, or until they paved the road

out and started widening the trails putting down
red gravel that absorbs and reflects the heat
and makes it too hot to hike even
in spring but the golden retriever and I

know back trails hidden that at times ramble off
property, but today we've come up on a
line of survey sticks and a line cut
deep into the woods. It doesn't do much

good, the survey line already cut, but I
pull up about twenty survey sticks far into
the woods self-righteous and smug, checking for
unwanted eyes, the dog wants to fetch them,

I dream I can stop fences and roads,
now they're all around the woods, I've been
caught in thunderstorms out here, the lightning crashing
all around, I've met up with snakes, deer,

wild pig, acquaintances that do not wish to
talk and strangers who will hike with you
with their dogs who will pack with mine
and become all joyful playful, I've picked up

on my portable short wave Christian fundamentalist remote
commune from New Mexico one Sunday singing songs
and their earnestness as beautiful as the trees
and another time with the short wave a

discussion from Greece in English of Henry Miller's
living in the islands, all while walking trails
twisting through yaupon and near tall sycamores though
I suffer from sleep apnea so some days

I wander trails muscles hurting from old age
and exhaustion the first miles but working the
pain out, though my mind, in exhaustion, is
a frozen block of emptiness that would make

the Buddhist proud, tinged with this sad strange
voice that whispers over and over, in my
head and out loud, 'I don't care, I
don't care,' it is the sensing of my

upcoming end the 'I don't care' and it
is good to say it to the sunlight
and the trees who in their indifference in
their other beauty do not care about my

At the Heart

exhaustion or pain, my weeks of no sleep
and I am glad that they don't care,
that they don't respond, that gives a certain
comfort and courage. Like large cities nature leaves

you alone and doesn't seem to give a
damn, lets you be, the dog and I
are coming up on a lake where I'll
throw a stick in the water and the

dog'll dive in to fetch the stick and
I know the dog's in a great blue
heaven when he swims out and clomps his
teeth around the stick, then turns and swims

toward shore, in heaven where all dogs go,
the ducks will fall like manna from the
sky into a lake as serene as this
and then the retrievers will bring them to

shore and when the dogs fetch another duck
the ones lying on the ground will resurrect
to fly again and years ago I found
at this rock ledge a pile of soccer

uniforms these boys had burned, then they built
a rope swing from a tree out over
the water and then they built a raft
to float on supported by large chunks of

Styrofoam. I know the boys were glad to
get away from civilization and parents, to find
a drop of freedom, but I knew they'd
get bored, my daughter swung on the swing

and went out on the raft before it
fell apart, a friend of mine and I
had to make several trips to pack out
in garbage bags all the ugly dirty floating

chunks of Styrofoam and restore the shore of
the lake, sometimes I'll find a lone fisherman
and we'll say howdy but even today with
all the development if I stay on the

old hidden back trails I may be out
there four, five hours and never see another
human soul, I used to grow quite proprietary
in the old days, somewhere deep inside I

held this place spiritually mine and forgot the
notion of the commons, saw myself as American
Zen Yamabushi, working the song lines of Lick
Creek, singing the land into being, recalling its

history, blessing with prayers, naming my and the
place's salvation, in solitude identifying with some crazy
higher inner self-purity; one spring Saturday I
came with the golden retriever, they were holding

some event, I don't remember what, I tried
to get away from the crowds, this lady
told me to get my dog on the
leash and for weeks my heart off balance

was disturbed, I'd lost my center, I was
dizzy, grumpy, busy moving around parts inside to
find the balance I'd lost, when I first
found these woods back in the late eighties

I'd bump sometimes into German tourists with binoculars,
serious birders, and it was salvation for me,
these woods, a kind of nearby paradise, an
image of something made from the ground up,

interdependence flowing to self-governance needing no lying
presidents or lords, kings or queens, and then
the beauty of it, especially the golden and
red browns of the waving blue stem of

At the Heart

autumn and winter, well it would just lift
me out of whatever the down I was
in, then I was still the solid romantic
who held that civilization was bad and that

nature was paradise—the good gods of the
incarnation right before your eyes, sure I'd read
a bit of Darwin and knew the competition
of species, but they're no bears, I wore

high boots for the copperheads, I wasn't on
anyone's food chain and carried a machete just
in case, I could look on the woods
and fields pictorially, see no deeper than the

skin of a painting's pigment on a wall
as I strode upright on trails observing and
musing, ah the beauty of it, strange colored
mushrooms and lichens on ravine rock damp, the

light on the lake, the giant trees down
in the bottoms by the old collapsed bridge,
the colors of the flitting flutterbys among the
spring wildflowers, one time I came the morning

following a huge hailstorm and the marble-sized
hail had drained in the hard rain, sailed
into depressions, where "clearies" of ice clustered like
diamonds; when you see something new in creation

you've never seen before, a song leaps inside,
a fire ignites, you know you'll never see
the natural miracle again, you feel your mortality
and yet are lifted, know what I mean,

when that new grace presents itself as an
unasked for but needed gift—ah but over
time, over years, these woods so special, so
poetic have become prosaic, prose, to me, and

Charles Taylor

now I can walk by these grasses and
trees with the same indifference I walk by
the windows full of glowing merchandise in the
mall that so enchants my teenage daughter who

no longer wishes to go hiking in the
woods, I don't get the re-creation from the
contrast with the city, the bang of difference,
ah the honeymoon is long gone but still

I come because I know all honeymoons go
and I am no longer the traveler seeking
the next honeymoon over the nearest horizon, I
try to travel well in my little Concord

in spite of the so called development and
my golden retriever Biscuit loves the woods so,
just today, as we reached the end of
the secret trail beyond the lake that moves

through thick woods to plunging ravines along Lick
Creek and comes out at a new bridge
leading in to a housing development, he found
part of a deer foreleg left behind by

a predator, I let him bring it back
to the pickup where he usually sits far
from me with his head out the window
but now he so enjoyed stretching out on

the seat with his front paws holding the
leg like a human clutching a drumstick on
Thanksgiving, gnawing the leg of the deer as
we drove back home and I've seen dead

deer along this road and have seen how
the circling turkey buzzards know to begin their
feast on the animal by going in through
the anus (much easier than through fur and

At the Heart

skin), I drive up to the now four
lane road beyond the new fire station to
where the freeway to Houston cuts through, amazed
at all this newness of construction. Some are

singing probably far away the making of big
dollars. They are I hope having fun and
we can't stop them, so far it doesn't
seem, in the climate change and the species

elimination. The story I've spun from letters may
one day slide away among the moldering leaves
of books asleep on the darkening shelves of
libraries forlorn and forgotten in a cauterized land.

The rich don't seem to care that in
time their taut dreams will be unstrung and
return to taunt them, that the arch of
human civil life will fall and nature'll sing

on free without our small revelations, making forest
after forest, sea after sea, in the sandy
soil my Golden and I've hiked ten years
at the place the county calls Lick Creek.

Charles Taylor

Like Washing the Dishes

Who digs for satori,
who drives their minds
like James Dean's jalopy
up to the cliff
seeking the IT, the
ALL, the Answer, the
Good, the God, the
Beautiful? Who drinks, who
dances, who shakes fists,
who shoots the mind
with music, with drugs,
with art, with hugs?
Not I said the
old man who sat
in the coffee shop.
I can look at
the wall or look
at the bright in
eyes, I can look
at this table light
or stare at my
shiny shoes when I'm
drowned by the blues.
I do not stall,
I flip the switch
inside my mind and
up and up and up
I go. I need
no blow to do
this show I tell
you true. I fly
this is no lie–
in the forest of
the soft rain in
the blue pure sky,
in the heart of
the heart, I fly.

Look Up

at night—
the moon,
the smoky
clouds, they
are saying
it all—
and in
the day
blue sky
green grass
at angle
with a
white simple
wall of
a country
church in
the sun
says it
all too.

Imagine
for John Lennon

Imagine you're standing next
to Russian genius novelist
Fyodor Dostoyevsky with the
other members of the
radical Petrashevsky group, about

to be shot by
fellow soldiers from your
own former military units.
You're pissing in your
pants, standing in the

December cold, shackled and
hooded; the priest, carrying
Bible and Cross, has
given God's blessing on
your death, the sentences

have been read, the
tall golden spire on
some church nearby has
gleamed in the clear
sunlight, Dostoyevsky has whispered,

"We'll be with Christ,"
and his friend Speshnev
has replied "A handful
of dust." The soldiers
take aim from fifteen

steps away from the
scaffolding, "I understood nothing
before I kissed the
cross," Dostoyevsky later said.
"They could not bring

themselves to trifle with
the cross." He remembers
Zola's *The Last Day
of a Condemned Man*,
and feels a profound

indifference to both life
or death. He thinks
how if he is
spared life would seem,
every second, endless, and

that would be unbearable.
Suddenly someone appears waving
a white cloth and
the soldiers lower their rifles.
A carriage clatters into

Semenovsky square, and a
sealed envelope from Adjutant
General Sumarkov is presented
and read. It is
the Czar's sudden pardon.

The joke's over. When
they untie Grigoryev, they
find he has gone
mad. The rest of
the prisoners feel nothing.

"They could just as
well as have shot
us," says Durov. Petrashevsky
demands not to be
touched, to put on

his own chains. He's
placed in a troika
and sent into a
life of endless exile.
Dostoyevsky gets four years

in a Siberian prison
and then must be,
till death, a soldier.
Later he is pardoned
and we have this

gift to the hearts
of all who love
to read and seek
wisdom. Imagine, when your
poor heart feels like

torn tarpaper; Imagine, when
you hear the killing
and torture; imagine and
learn to dwell in
a hope not born

and imagine what Jack
wrote to Joyce from
the Slovenia headed for
Tangiers. The ship nearly
floundered in mountainous waves

five hundred miles out.
Jack discovered inside a
luminous calm and wrote:
EVERYTHING IS GOD, NOTHING
EVER HAPPENED EXCEPT GOD.

Again, the Brazos Valley

You slaves right here
I feel you near
Around my insomnia bed
We make a web

The cotton came down
Down from around Waco
Down from around Calvert
Down from around Cameron

The cotton came down
First on the river
First on the Brazos
Then on the trains

On the railroad cars
The cotton came down
The slaves sweating in
The cauterizing summer heat

Moving row to row
The slaves sweating in
The summer cauterizing heat
Moving row by row

Pulling the sharp balls
From the brown plants
Blood and cutting of fingers
Pulling the black seeds

From white cotton crowns
Loading the cotton on trains
Loading the cotton in cars
Bundled, headed for Galveston

Compressed perhaps, then loaded
On large sailing ships
Loaded on metal ships
For the English mills

For the cotton mills
Children at the bobbins
Making the worlds' clothes
Sixty hours a week

From Galveston cotton warehouses
Only recently torn down
But you slaves here
From many unmarked graves

Whisper names in my ear
I feel you near
We know the fear
and hear the tears

All around my bed
Where pain can't ebb
Till you are honored
And the names read

Let it be said
For those held dear
For all who bled
So we're all fed

And can move clear
In the holy web
Where cotton came down
Where cotton came down

Clouds
For Melissa Studdard

So I say if they give you lemons that taste like nails
You might go ahead and make somber battery acid

So I say if they pave over those trees you so dearly
loved, that dense forest of hardwoods that ran

along the flood plain of Wolf Pen Creek, to build
a line of commonplace chain corporate eateries

that drove out of business the local establishments,
then I say this time take time to consider not

taking acid revenge, don't give yourself an ulcer
or disfigure anyone's face. Go out and consider

the quiet clouds, they haven't found a way to market
the clouds yet, no one as yet claims mineral rights

or owns the deeds to clouds. So I say stare at
the common clouds, watch them drift across the

sagacious empty blue of sky, using a tree perhaps
as your reference point, and enjoy the way

the clouds shape-shift, how they build cathedrals
way up in the air and then break them silently

down right in the soft miles before your eyes,
watch till time grows timeless and the sun

begins to set and you see how the rosy fingers of
the sun illuminate the clouds at first, but

then the color shifts, taking on bands of purple
or yellow tone, and then the sun sets further

and its light just clips the lower bumps of clouds,
making them a pinkish orange, while the

rest of the clouds grow dark. Your soul is like
those clouds. Luminous and light your soul

shape-shifts through the sky of your body, building
splendid architectures, taking on such holy

colors. Timeless are the clouds of your unknowing
where the worries of naming lemon words

break like a mirror dropped on a floor and your
humble rosy heart drifts in a living peace on its

royal road to falling snow or blessing rain. That's
you, you know, sliding so easy from life to life

Charles Taylor has published two novels, *Drifter's Story* and *Fogg in High School*, and also three short story collections, *Lights of the City*, *Somebody to Love*, and *It All Flows Away*. His has recently published two poetry collections, *Heterosexual: A Love Story* (Panther Creek Press), and *Like Li-Po Laughing at the Lonely Moon* (Pecan Grove Press). His most recent title is a memoir from Four Genres Press called *Saving Sebastan: A Father's Journey through his Son's Drug Abuse*.

Taylor has worked as a bookstore clerk, children's magician, balloon clown, survey taker, janitor, soft water salesman, maintenance man, and animal lab assistant. He's also worked for in the National Endowment's CETA Artist Program, the Poets-in-the School's Program, and taught at Angelo State University and the Universities of Texas at Tyler, El Paso, and Austin. In the early 1990's, inspired by his poet mentor Lucien Stryk and by Gary Snyder, Taylor moved to Japan to teach and become more engaged in Asian aesthetics.

For the last two decades he has taught creative writing, film, American nature writing, and the Beat Movement in American literature at Texas A&M University in College Station. He's married to Takako Saito and has three children Will, James, and Lisa. You can reach the author here:
"Chuck Taylor" <mysticpoetics@gmail.com>

CPSIA information can be obtained at www.ICGtesting.com
Printed in the USA
LVOW120831211212

312649LV00001B/48/P